Of Land And Sea
A Kid's Guide To Trapani, Sicily, Italy

Photography by John D. Weigand
Poetry by Penelope Dyan

Bellissima Publishing, LLC
Jamul, California
www.bellissimapublishing.com

Copyright © 2016 by Penny D. Weigand and John D. Weigand

All rights reserved. No part of this book may be reproduced or transmitted in any form or by any means, electronic or mechanical, including photocopying, recording, or by any other means, or by any information or storage retrieval system, without permission from the publisher.

ISBN 978-1-61477-261-3
First Edition

"Philosophy begins in wonder."

PLATO

Of Land And Sea
Bellissima Publishing, LLC

Introduction

Trapani is a city in Sicily, Italy that was founded way back in time by a group of people called the Elymians. Their Iron age history is basically the same as that of their nearby Sicani neighbors; and they adopted the Greek alphabet into their own language, a language no one has been able to translate to this day. Some Sicilians will tell you they are the same as the Greeks, probably because their histories intertwine.

Much of the old city of Trapani dates from the late medieval or early modern period, and Fishing and canning are the main local industries. There is a lot to see and do in Trapani, and many things will catch your eye. This is truly one place where the sky meets the sea, and it's a great place to be! So bring your walking shoes and your camera and take pictures of your own as you do a great explore! Mainly, think about the past, the present and the future and how the people intermingled cultures, just as everyone has done since the beginning of time, to create the great, vast world in which we live today. This learn to read' book gives you a peek at what you can see in Trapani, and in the hills of Erice. And be sure to watch the free music video on the Bellissimavideo YouTube channel to see even more of this city!

Of Land And Sea
Bellissima Publishing, LLC

Of Land And Sea
A Kid's Guide To Trapani, Sicily, Italy

Photography by John D. Weigand
Poetry by Penelope Dyan

With the sky overhead,
the bluest of blue,
the Sicilian city of Trapini (in Italy)
calls out to you!

High on a hill is Erice,
where the SKY reaches down
to meet the wondrous sea.
It's a beautiful sight,
as beautiful as can be!
Yes, right below you will discover
a panorama unfurled,
as you sit looking down
from on top of the world!

And the Mediterranean Sea,
looks ever so blue,
that you wonder if what you see
can truly be true.
You wonder, "Are my eyes simply
playing tricks on me,
as I look down to where
the LAND now meets the sea?"

And as you look down again
at the harbor,
your mother says,
"Yes, it is true.
The sky and the water right here
(and right now)
are REALLY that blue!"

And so you look and you observe,
because you want to see
what you can see,
and hear ALL that can be heard.

The worn streets remind you
of things now long past,
of wars and of great tribulations,
and of things meant to last,
like warmth and goodness,
kindness and light,
like the love of your mother,
as she tucks you into bed each night!

Next, you see puppets, toys and fun,
Mom says, "Get ready!
The time for shopping has begun!"
Then Dad lets out one great big sigh.
But he knows better
that to tell Mom NOT TO SHOP,
so he won't EVEN try!

There are postcards
and other paper things
meant to capture forever
the memories this place brings.

There are healthy snacks to eat,
like oranges, a fruit, juicy and sweet!

There are toys and souvenirs,
and there is even more . . .

Your mom can buy ceramics galore!

As you remember that Erice church,
Chiesa Madre, so regal and so old,
you know that about THIS place
there must be many stories to be told.
And you think to yourself,
that one place is not just like another,
as you look up and smile
at your dear, sweet mother.

You have soaked up some history,
and you have learned quite a lot.
And it seems for all our differences,
the world is STILL a melting pot!
To Trapani came the Elymians,
the Greeks, the Arabs, the French
and the conquerors from Rome,
all coming together
to claim THIS place as home.
And as you walk through the arch
and into into the city's light,
somehow you know it's ALL just right!
Here, the sky and land meet the sea!
It's exactly as it was intended to be!

"You should always look to the horizon, because that's where the sky always meets the sea."

PENELOPE DYAN